Christmas 2015

Fiona,

Look for the stars that shine in your heart!

Shine On Always,
Nancy Godbout Jurica

Bright Star of Palmer Lake

Late in the afternoon, when dusk
begins and winter daylight fades
into aspen and pine, a quiet snow
dusts the rooftops, settles like thin sugar
in cathedrals of red rock as the slow 5:10
coal train meanders by the silent lake.

A small Colorado town welcomes December
with a star shining from the mountainside.
For generations this sparkling tradition
offers a beacon for the weary traveler,
with the comfort of returning home
where warmth waits like a soft weathered quilt.

The night wind's bright music weaves
pure harmonies from bough to bough.
A family pauses in the cold to listen
to the celestial symphony heard only
on this hillside where heaven's candlelight
shines out for miles to the hungry hearts of mankind.

Nancy Godbout Jurka 2015
Kay LaBella

DEDICATION

To my husband, Atis
My sons, Aaron & Andrew Jurka
-NGJ

To my mother, Pat Petrocine
To my children, Corinne, Luke & Connor LaBella
-KLB

And to all children past, present and future of Palmer Lake, Colorado.

It is our hope that this book inspires magical memories of the Palmer Lake Star.
-Nancy Godbout Jurka & Kay La Bella

-First Edition-

ISBN 978-0-9969035-0-9

Library of Congress Control Number
2015917129

10 9 8 7 6 5 4 3 2 1

Text Copyright ©2012 by Nancy Godbout Jurka   Cover art and interior illustrations by Kay LaBella ©2015
Cover and interior design by Andrew Blake Jurka, Mountain Tapestry Press
Photography by Aaron Atis Jurka, Mountain Tapestry Press

All rights reserved. Published in the United States by
Mountain Tapestry Press, LLC Palmer Lake, Colorado.

MountainTapestryPress.com

This book may not be reproduced in whole or part in any form or by any means, electronic
or mechanical now known or hereafter invented, without the expressed written permission
of the publisher.
Manufactured in the United States of America

Nancy Godbout Jurka Kay LaBella

Bright Star of Palmer Lake

late in the afternoon, when dusk begins and waits

daylight fades into aspen and pine

A quiet snow dusts the rooftops,

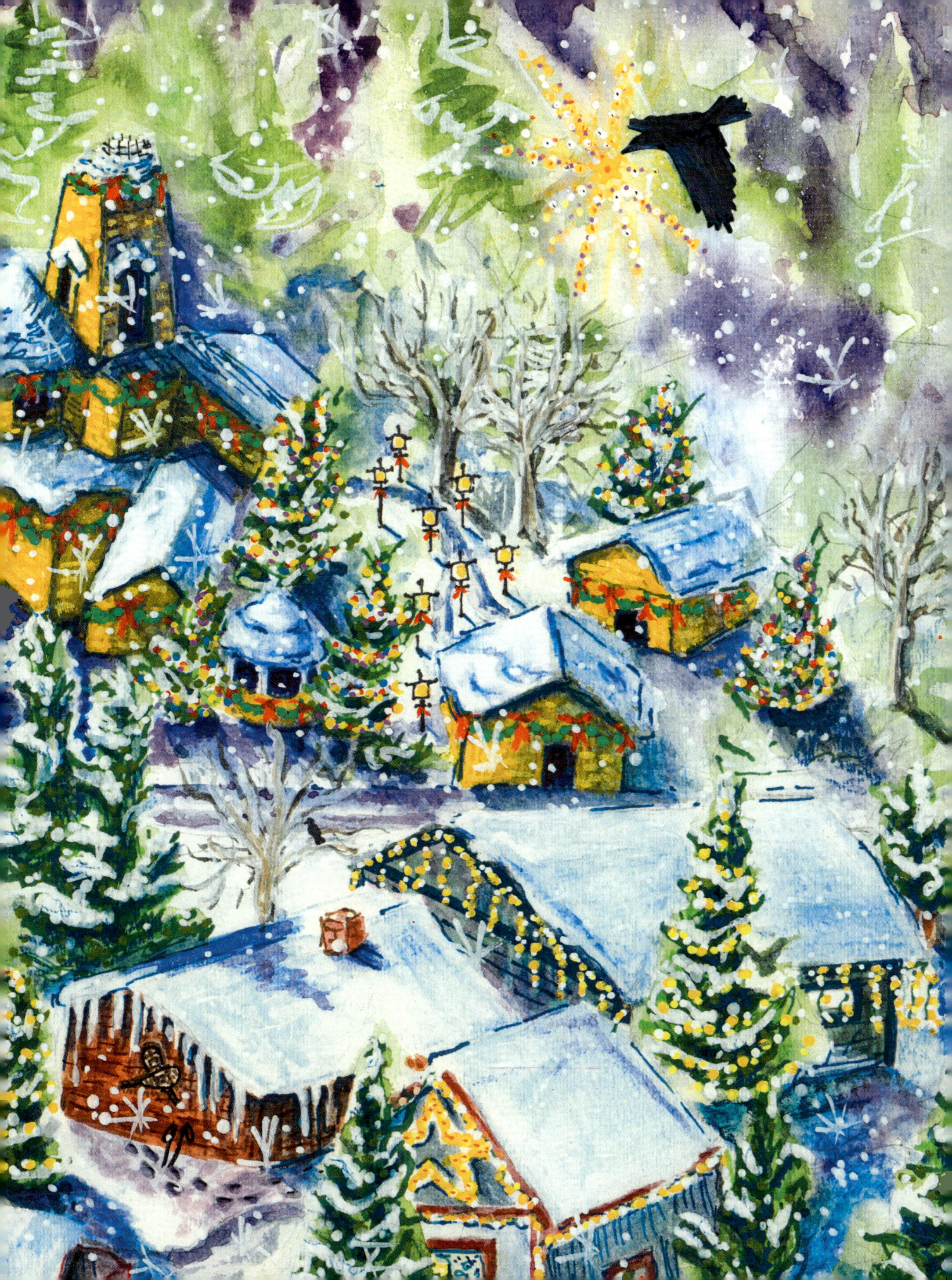

...settles like thin sugar

in Cathedrals of red rock

...........as the slow 5:10 coal train

meanders by the silent lake.

A small Colorado town welcomes December with a ⭐

Shining from the Mountain Side

FOR GENERATIONS

HIS * SPARKLING * TRADITION

offers a BEACON

for the weary traveler.

With the Comfort

of returning Home.

Where Warmth Waits

like a soft weathered quilt.

The Night winds' Bright Music weaves pure Harmonies

from Bough to Bough

A family pauses in the cold to listen

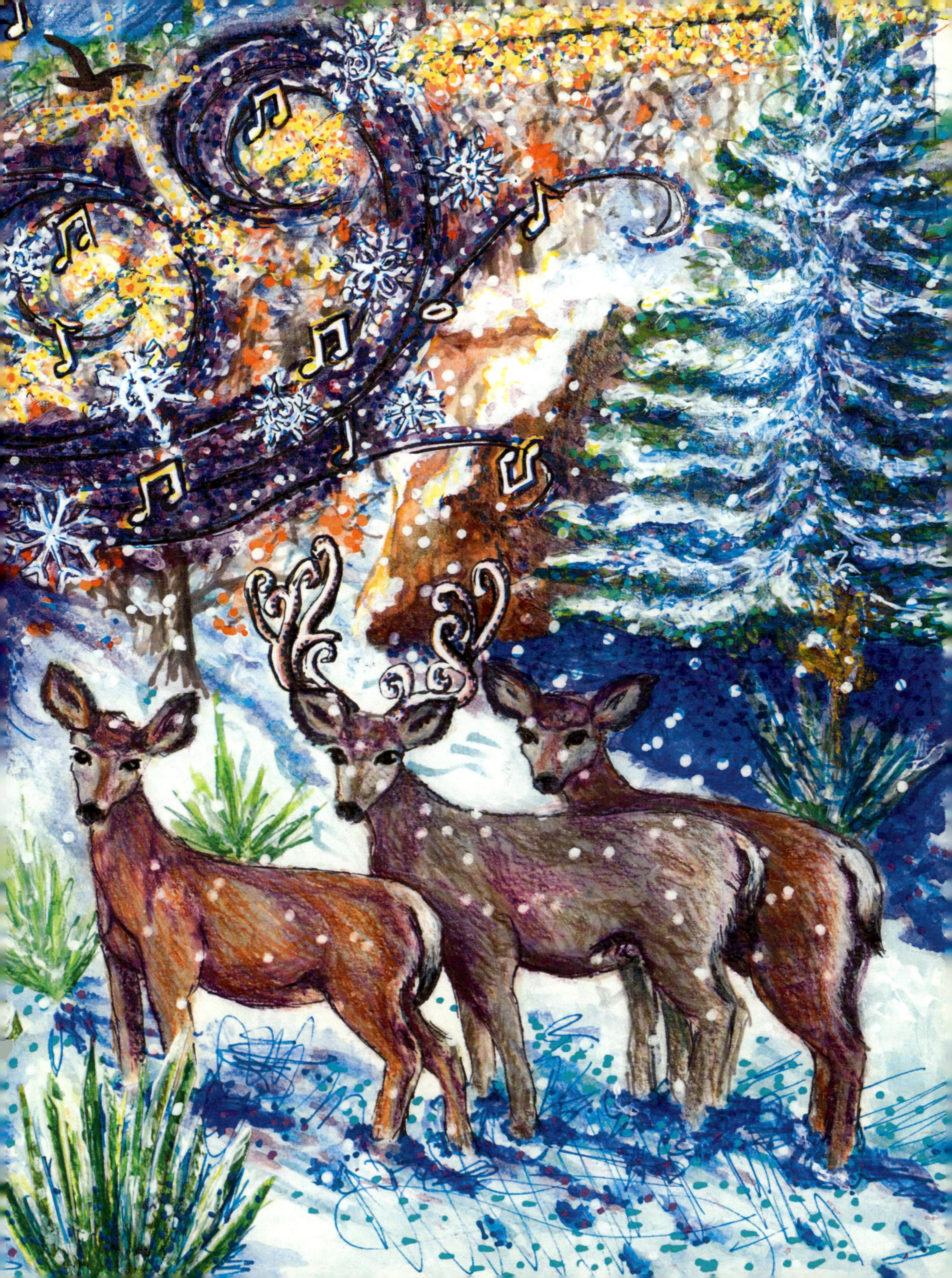

to the celestial symphony

heard only on this hillside

where heaven's candlelight shines out for miles

to the hungry hearts of mankind.

Nancy Godbout Jurka, the author of numerous poems, has lived in Colorado for more than thirty years. She is best known for her poetry collection, *Journey On: Beauty and Grit Along the Way*. Born in West Point, New York, she graduated from Mount Saint Mary College and is retired from a career in elementary and special education. An avid gardener and traveler, Nancy lives in Palmer Lake, Colorado with her husband and family. *Bright Star of Palmer Lake* is her first illustrated poetry book.

Kay La Bella, the illustrator graduated from Colorado State University and later received her MFA from LaCrosse University. A retired Art/Science teacher who now resides in Colorado Springs, she loves exploring the creative arts and teaching private lessons. Kay, who raised her three children in Palmer Lake, has a love of gardening, hiking and mountain biking with her dog Cado, and takes road trips as often as possible. *Bright Star of Palmer Lake* is her first illustrated book.

Photo courtesy of Aaron Atis Jurka

History of the Palmer Lake Star

In the summer of 1935, a group of citizens from Palmer Lake, Colorado, introduced the idea of a lighted star on the mountainside that could be seen for miles during the upcoming Christmas season. Originally known as "The Star of Bethlehem", it was the town's contribution to cheer up its citizens and to show America's courage and determination during the Depression Era. Eighty years later, the Palmer Lake Star continues to shine throughout December and on another special occasions such as Memorial Day and the Fourth of July. Composed of ninety-one high efficiency LED lights, it stands more than 400 feet tall and wide. This beloved star is visible to travelers between Colorado Springs and Denver. In January 2013, the Palmer Lake Star was listed on the Colorado State Register of Historic Properties.

Source: Jack Anthony, Palmer Lake Star Historian